50 Simple Desserts with Five Ingredients or Less

By: Kelly Johnson

Table of Contents

- Chocolate Covered Strawberries
- Banana Ice Cream
- Peanut Butter Cookies
- Rice Krispie Treats
- Nutella Mug Cake
- Oreo Truffles
- Coconut Macaroons
- Lemon Sorbet
- Chia Seed Pudding
- Apple Nachos
- Frozen Grapes
- Chocolate Mousse
- Baked Apples
- Pineapple Whip
- Pumpkin Mousse
- Berry Parfait
- Chocolate-Covered Bananas
- Mini Cheesecakes
- Fruit Salad
- No-Bake Energy Bites
- Peanut Butter Fudge
- Chocolate Bark
- Mango Sorbet
- Coffee Granita
- Nutella Banana Quesadilla
- Caramelized Bananas
- S'mores Dip
- Strawberry Shortcake
- Jelly Cups
- Chocolate Coconut Truffles
- Graham Cracker Pudding
- Cinnamon Sugar Tortilla Chips
- Frozen Yogurt Bark
- Cherry Crisp
- Vanilla Pudding
- Meringue Cookies

- Pudding Cups
- Chocolate Chip Cookie Dough Bites
- No-Bake Cheesecake
- Fruit Sorbet
- Almond Joy Energy Bites
- Peanut Butter Banana Bites
- Chocolate Avocado Mousse
- Honey Yogurt with Nuts
- Peanut Butter Rice Cakes
- Chocolate Hazelnut Spread on Toast
- Strawberry Ice Cream
- Maple Syrup Pecan Clusters
- Mocha Chocolate Cups
- Sliced Pears with Honey

Chocolate Covered Strawberries

Ingredients

- 1 pound fresh strawberries, washed and dried
- 8 ounces dark chocolate, chopped
- 1 tablespoon coconut oil (optional)

Instructions

1. Melt the dark chocolate and coconut oil (if using) in a microwave-safe bowl in 30-second intervals, stirring in between, until smooth.
2. Dip each strawberry into the melted chocolate, allowing any excess to drip off.
3. Place the chocolate-covered strawberries on a parchment-lined baking sheet.
4. Refrigerate for at least 30 minutes until the chocolate is set.

Banana Ice Cream

Ingredients

- 4 ripe bananas, sliced and frozen
- Optional add-ins: vanilla extract, cocoa powder, or peanut butter

Instructions

1. Place the frozen banana slices in a food processor and blend until smooth and creamy, scraping down the sides as needed.
2. If desired, add any optional ingredients and blend again until combined.
3. Serve immediately for a soft-serve texture, or freeze for an additional hour for a firmer consistency.

Peanut Butter Cookies

Ingredients

- 1 cup creamy peanut butter
- 1 cup brown sugar
- 1 egg
- 1 teaspoon vanilla extract
- 1/2 teaspoon baking soda

Instructions

1. Preheat the oven to 350°F (175°C).
2. In a mixing bowl, combine peanut butter, brown sugar, egg, vanilla extract, and baking soda. Mix until well combined.
3. Roll the dough into balls and place them on a parchment-lined baking sheet. Flatten each ball with a fork.
4. Bake for 10-12 minutes until the edges are set. Let cool on the baking sheet for a few minutes before transferring to a wire rack.

Rice Krispie Treats

Ingredients

- 6 cups Rice Krispies cereal
- 4 cups mini marshmallows
- 3 tablespoons butter

Instructions

1. In a large saucepan, melt the butter over low heat. Add the mini marshmallows and stir until melted and smooth.
2. Remove from heat and stir in the Rice Krispies cereal until evenly coated.
3. Press the mixture into a greased 9x13-inch baking dish. Let cool before cutting into squares.

Nutella Mug Cake

Ingredients

- 4 tablespoons all-purpose flour
- 4 tablespoons sugar
- 2 tablespoons cocoa powder
- 1/8 teaspoon baking powder
- 3 tablespoons milk
- 2 tablespoons Nutella
- 1 tablespoon vegetable oil
- Optional: chocolate chips or nuts

Instructions

1. In a microwave-safe mug, mix the flour, sugar, cocoa powder, and baking powder.
2. Add the milk, Nutella, and vegetable oil, stirring until smooth.
3. If desired, stir in chocolate chips or nuts.
4. Microwave on high for 1 minute and 30 seconds, or until the cake is set. Allow to cool slightly before enjoying.

Oreo Truffles

Ingredients

- 1 package (15.35 ounces) Oreo cookies
- 8 ounces cream cheese, softened
- 8 ounces chocolate (dark, milk, or white) for coating

Instructions

1. Crush the Oreo cookies into fine crumbs in a food processor.
2. In a bowl, mix the cookie crumbs with softened cream cheese until well combined.
3. Roll the mixture into small balls and place them on a parchment-lined baking sheet.
4. Melt the chocolate and dip each truffle, then return them to the baking sheet. Refrigerate until set.

Coconut Macaroons

Ingredients

- 3 cups shredded coconut
- 1/2 cup sweetened condensed milk
- 1 teaspoon vanilla extract
- Optional: melted chocolate for drizzling

Instructions

1. Preheat the oven to 325°F (165°C).
2. In a bowl, combine shredded coconut, sweetened condensed milk, and vanilla extract until well mixed.
3. Scoop spoonfuls of the mixture onto a parchment-lined baking sheet.
4. Bake for 15-20 minutes until golden brown. Let cool before drizzling with melted chocolate, if desired.

Lemon Sorbet

Ingredients

- 1 cup water
- 1 cup sugar
- 1 cup fresh lemon juice (about 4-6 lemons)
- Zest of 1 lemon

Instructions

1. In a saucepan, combine water and sugar over medium heat. Stir until the sugar is dissolved. Remove from heat and let cool.
2. Add the lemon juice and lemon zest to the sugar water and mix well.
3. Pour the mixture into an ice cream maker and churn according to the manufacturer's instructions. If you don't have an ice cream maker, pour the mixture into a shallow dish and freeze, stirring every 30 minutes until frozen.

Chia Seed Pudding

Ingredients

- 1/4 cup chia seeds
- 1 cup milk (dairy or non-dairy)
- 1 tablespoon honey or maple syrup
- Optional toppings: fruit, nuts, or granola

Instructions

1. In a bowl, combine chia seeds, milk, and honey or maple syrup. Stir well to combine.
2. Refrigerate for at least 4 hours or overnight until thickened.
3. Stir again before serving and top with your choice of fruit, nuts, or granola.

Apple Nachos

Ingredients

- 2 large apples, cored and sliced
- 1/4 cup peanut butter or almond butter
- 1/4 cup granola
- 1/4 cup mini chocolate chips
- Optional toppings: shredded coconut, chopped nuts, or drizzled honey

Instructions

1. Arrange the apple slices on a large plate or serving platter.
2. Drizzle the peanut butter over the apple slices.
3. Sprinkle granola and mini chocolate chips on top.
4. Add any additional toppings you like and serve immediately.

Frozen Grapes

Ingredients

- 2 cups seedless grapes, washed and dried

Instructions

1. Place the grapes in a single layer on a baking sheet.
2. Freeze the grapes for at least 2 hours or until frozen solid.
3. Serve as a refreshing snack straight from the freezer.

Chocolate Mousse

Ingredients

- 6 ounces semi-sweet chocolate, chopped
- 3 tablespoons unsalted butter
- 2 large eggs, separated
- 1/4 cup sugar
- 1 cup heavy whipping cream

Instructions

1. Melt the chocolate and butter in a heatproof bowl set over simmering water. Remove from heat and let cool slightly.
2. Whisk the egg yolks and sugar together until pale and thick, then stir into the cooled chocolate mixture.
3. In another bowl, beat the egg whites until soft peaks form. Gently fold the egg whites into the chocolate mixture.
4. In a separate bowl, whip the heavy cream until soft peaks form, then fold it into the chocolate mixture until smooth.
5. Spoon the mousse into individual serving dishes and refrigerate for at least 2 hours before serving.

Baked Apples

Ingredients

- 4 medium apples, cored
- 1/4 cup brown sugar
- 1 teaspoon cinnamon
- 1/4 cup raisins or walnuts (optional)
- 1/4 cup water

Instructions

1. Preheat the oven to 350°F (175°C).
2. In a bowl, mix brown sugar, cinnamon, and optional raisins or walnuts.
3. Stuff the mixture into the cored apples and place them in a baking dish.
4. Pour water into the dish and cover with foil.
5. Bake for 25-30 minutes, until the apples are tender. Serve warm.

Pineapple Whip

Ingredients

- 2 cups frozen pineapple chunks
- 1 cup coconut milk (or vanilla yogurt)

Instructions

1. In a blender, combine the frozen pineapple and coconut milk.
2. Blend until smooth and creamy.
3. Serve immediately as a soft-serve treat, or freeze for a firmer texture.

Pumpkin Mousse

Ingredients

- 1 cup canned pumpkin puree
- 1/2 cup heavy cream
- 1/2 cup powdered sugar
- 1 teaspoon pumpkin pie spice
- 1 teaspoon vanilla extract

Instructions

1. In a bowl, whip the heavy cream and powdered sugar until soft peaks form.
2. In another bowl, mix the pumpkin puree, pumpkin pie spice, and vanilla extract until smooth.
3. Gently fold the whipped cream into the pumpkin mixture until combined.
4. Spoon into serving dishes and refrigerate for at least 1 hour before serving.

Berry Parfait

Ingredients

- 2 cups mixed berries (strawberries, blueberries, raspberries)
- 2 cups yogurt (Greek or regular)
- 1/2 cup granola
- Honey or maple syrup (optional)

Instructions

1. In a glass or bowl, layer yogurt, mixed berries, and granola.
2. Repeat layers until all ingredients are used.
3. Drizzle with honey or maple syrup if desired and serve immediately.

Chocolate-Covered Bananas

Ingredients

- 2 ripe bananas, sliced
- 1 cup dark chocolate chips
- 1 tablespoon coconut oil (optional)

Instructions

1. Melt the chocolate chips and coconut oil (if using) in a microwave-safe bowl, stirring every 30 seconds until smooth.
2. Dip each banana slice into the melted chocolate, allowing excess to drip off.
3. Place the chocolate-covered bananas on a parchment-lined baking sheet and freeze until set, about 30 minutes. Enjoy frozen or chilled.

Mini Cheesecakes

Ingredients

- 1 cup graham cracker crumbs
- 1/4 cup sugar
- 1/2 cup unsalted butter, melted
- 16 ounces cream cheese, softened
- 1/2 cup sugar
- 1 teaspoon vanilla extract
- 2 large eggs

Instructions

1. Preheat the oven to 325°F (160°C). Line a muffin tin with paper liners.
2. In a bowl, combine graham cracker crumbs, sugar, and melted butter. Press the mixture into the bottom of each liner to form the crust.
3. In another bowl, beat cream cheese, sugar, and vanilla until smooth. Add eggs one at a time, mixing until just combined.
4. Pour the cheesecake filling over the crusts, filling each liner about 3/4 full.
5. Bake for 20-25 minutes, until set. Allow to cool, then refrigerate for at least 2 hours before serving.

Fruit Salad

Ingredients

- 2 cups strawberries, hulled and sliced
- 2 cups blueberries
- 2 cups pineapple, diced
- 2 cups kiwi, peeled and sliced
- Juice of 1 lime
- 2 tablespoons honey (optional)

Instructions

1. In a large bowl, combine all the fruit.
2. Drizzle lime juice and honey over the fruit and gently toss to combine.
3. Serve immediately or refrigerate until ready to serve.

No-Bake Energy Bites

Ingredients

- 1 cup rolled oats
- 1/2 cup peanut butter
- 1/3 cup honey
- 1/2 cup chocolate chips
- 1/2 cup ground flaxseed
- 1 teaspoon vanilla extract

Instructions

1. In a bowl, mix all ingredients until well combined.
2. Roll the mixture into small balls and place on a baking sheet.
3. Refrigerate for at least 30 minutes to firm up. Store in the refrigerator.

Peanut Butter Fudge

Ingredients

- 1 cup peanut butter
- 1/2 cup unsalted butter
- 3 cups powdered sugar
- 1 teaspoon vanilla extract

Instructions

1. In a saucepan, melt peanut butter and butter over low heat.
2. Stir in powdered sugar and vanilla until smooth.
3. Pour the mixture into a greased 8x8-inch pan and spread evenly.
4. Refrigerate until firm, about 2 hours. Cut into squares before serving.

Chocolate Bark

Ingredients

- 2 cups dark chocolate chips
- 1/2 cup nuts (almonds, walnuts, or pistachios), chopped
- 1/2 cup dried fruit (cranberries or apricots), chopped
- Sea salt (optional)

Instructions

1. Melt chocolate chips in a microwave-safe bowl, stirring every 30 seconds until smooth.
2. Spread the melted chocolate onto a parchment-lined baking sheet.
3. Sprinkle with nuts, dried fruit, and sea salt if desired.
4. Refrigerate until set, then break into pieces.

Mango Sorbet

Ingredients

- 2 ripe mangoes, peeled and diced
- 1/2 cup sugar
- 1 tablespoon lime juice

Instructions

1. In a blender, combine mango, sugar, and lime juice. Blend until smooth.
2. Pour the mixture into a shallow dish and freeze for about 2 hours.
3. Scrape with a fork to create a fluffy texture, then serve immediately or store in the freezer.

Coffee Granita

Ingredients

- 2 cups brewed coffee, cooled
- 1/2 cup sugar
- 1 teaspoon vanilla extract

Instructions

1. In a bowl, mix coffee, sugar, and vanilla until sugar is dissolved.
2. Pour the mixture into a shallow dish and freeze for 1 hour.
3. After an hour, use a fork to scrape the ice crystals. Return to the freezer and repeat every 30 minutes until fluffy.
4. Serve in cups or bowls.

Nutella Banana Quesadilla

Ingredients

- 2 large flour tortillas
- 1/2 cup Nutella
- 1 banana, sliced
- 1/4 cup mini marshmallows (optional)
- Cooking spray or butter for grilling

Instructions

1. Spread Nutella over one side of each tortilla.
2. Layer banana slices and marshmallows (if using) on one tortilla, then top with the second tortilla, Nutella side down.
3. Heat a skillet over medium heat and lightly grease it. Cook the quesadilla for 2-3 minutes on each side, until golden brown.
4. Cut into wedges and serve warm.

Caramelized Bananas

Ingredients

- 4 ripe bananas, sliced
- 1/4 cup brown sugar
- 2 tablespoons unsalted butter
- 1 teaspoon cinnamon
- 1 tablespoon lemon juice

Instructions

1. In a large skillet over medium heat, melt the butter.
2. Add the brown sugar and cinnamon, stirring until combined.
3. Add the banana slices and cook for 2-3 minutes on each side, until caramelized.
4. Drizzle with lemon juice before serving. Enjoy warm over ice cream or on its own!

S'mores Dip

Ingredients

- 1 cup chocolate chips (milk or dark)
- 1 cup mini marshmallows
- Graham crackers, for dipping

Instructions

1. Preheat the oven to 450°F (230°C).
2. In a cast-iron skillet or oven-safe dish, layer the chocolate chips and top with mini marshmallows.
3. Bake for 5-7 minutes, until the marshmallows are golden brown.
4. Serve immediately with graham crackers for dipping.

Strawberry Shortcake

Ingredients

- 2 cups strawberries, hulled and sliced
- 1/4 cup sugar
- 1 cup heavy cream
- 1 tablespoon vanilla extract
- 1 pound shortcake or sponge cake, cut into slices

Instructions

1. In a bowl, combine sliced strawberries and sugar. Let sit for 15 minutes to release juices.
2. In another bowl, whip heavy cream with vanilla until soft peaks form.
3. To assemble, layer shortcake with strawberries and whipped cream. Serve immediately.

Jelly Cups

Ingredients

- 2 cups fruit juice (your choice)
- 1/2 cup water
- 1 packet gelatin (or agar-agar for a vegetarian option)
- Fresh fruit, for garnish (optional)

Instructions

1. In a saucepan, heat water until just boiling. Remove from heat and stir in gelatin until dissolved.
2. Add fruit juice and mix well. Pour into cups or molds.
3. Refrigerate until set, about 4 hours. Garnish with fresh fruit if desired.

Chocolate Coconut Truffles

Ingredients

- 1 cup dark chocolate chips
- 1/2 cup sweetened shredded coconut
- 1/4 cup coconut cream
- 1 teaspoon vanilla extract

Instructions

1. In a microwave-safe bowl, melt chocolate chips until smooth.
2. Stir in coconut cream and vanilla extract until well combined.
3. Refrigerate for about 30 minutes until firm enough to handle.
4. Scoop out small portions and roll into balls, then roll in shredded coconut to coat.

Graham Cracker Pudding

Ingredients

- 2 cups milk
- 1/4 cup sugar
- 2 tablespoons cornstarch
- 1 teaspoon vanilla extract
- 1 cup crushed graham crackers
- Whipped cream, for topping

Instructions

1. In a saucepan, combine milk, sugar, and cornstarch over medium heat. Stir until thickened.
2. Remove from heat and stir in vanilla extract and crushed graham crackers.
3. Pour into serving cups and refrigerate until chilled. Top with whipped cream before serving.

Cinnamon Sugar Tortilla Chips

Ingredients

- 4 flour tortillas
- 1/4 cup melted butter
- 1/4 cup sugar
- 1 tablespoon cinnamon

Instructions

1. Preheat the oven to 350°F (175°C).
2. Cut tortillas into triangles and arrange on a baking sheet.
3. Brush with melted butter and sprinkle with a mixture of sugar and cinnamon.
4. Bake for 10-12 minutes until golden brown and crispy. Let cool before serving.

Frozen Yogurt Bark

Ingredients

- 2 cups Greek yogurt (plain or flavored)
- 1/4 cup honey or maple syrup
- 1 cup mixed berries (fresh or frozen)
- 1/4 cup nuts or granola (optional)

Instructions

1. Line a baking sheet with parchment paper.
2. In a bowl, mix yogurt and honey until well combined.
3. Spread the yogurt mixture onto the prepared baking sheet in an even layer.
4. Sprinkle with berries and nuts or granola. Freeze for 4 hours or until solid.
5. Break into pieces and serve frozen.

Cherry Crisp

Ingredients

- 4 cups fresh or frozen cherries, pitted
- 1 cup oats
- 1/2 cup brown sugar
- 1/3 cup all-purpose flour
- 1 teaspoon cinnamon
- 1/4 cup unsalted butter, melted

Instructions

1. Preheat the oven to 350°F (175°C).
2. In a bowl, mix cherries with 1/4 cup of brown sugar and set aside.
3. In another bowl, combine oats, remaining brown sugar, flour, cinnamon, and melted butter.
4. Spread the cherries in a baking dish and top with the oat mixture.
5. Bake for 30-35 minutes until the topping is golden brown. Serve warm.

Vanilla Pudding

Ingredients

- 2 cups milk
- 1/2 cup sugar
- 1/4 cup cornstarch
- 1/4 teaspoon salt
- 1 tablespoon vanilla extract
- 2 tablespoons butter

Instructions

1. In a saucepan, whisk together milk, sugar, cornstarch, and salt. Cook over medium heat, stirring constantly, until thickened.
2. Remove from heat and stir in vanilla extract and butter until smooth.
3. Pour into serving cups and chill in the refrigerator until set.

Meringue Cookies

Ingredients

- 4 large egg whites
- 1 cup granulated sugar
- 1/4 teaspoon cream of tartar
- 1 teaspoon vanilla extract

Instructions

1. Preheat the oven to 225°F (110°C) and line a baking sheet with parchment paper.
2. In a mixing bowl, beat egg whites until soft peaks form. Gradually add sugar and cream of tartar, continuing to beat until stiff peaks form.
3. Gently fold in vanilla extract.
4. Spoon or pipe the meringue onto the prepared baking sheet.
5. Bake for 1 hour until dry and crisp. Turn off the oven and let meringues cool completely inside.

Pudding Cups

Ingredients

- 2 cups chocolate or vanilla pudding (store-bought or homemade)
- 1/2 cup crushed graham crackers
- 1/4 cup whipped cream
- Chocolate shavings or fruit, for garnish

Instructions

1. In serving cups, layer chocolate or vanilla pudding at the bottom.
2. Add a layer of crushed graham crackers, followed by whipped cream.
3. Repeat the layers as desired and top with chocolate shavings or fruit. Chill before serving.

Chocolate Chip Cookie Dough Bites

Ingredients

- 1/2 cup unsalted butter, softened
- 1/2 cup brown sugar
- 1/4 cup granulated sugar
- 1 teaspoon vanilla extract
- 1 cup all-purpose flour (heat-treated)
- 1/2 cup chocolate chips
- Pinch of salt

Instructions

1. In a mixing bowl, cream together butter, brown sugar, granulated sugar, and vanilla until smooth.
2. Gradually mix in flour and salt, then fold in chocolate chips.
3. Roll into small balls and place on a baking sheet. Chill until firm.

No-Bake Cheesecake

Ingredients

- 8 oz cream cheese, softened
- 1/2 cup powdered sugar
- 1 teaspoon vanilla extract
- 1 cup heavy cream, whipped
- 1 graham cracker crust

Instructions

1. In a bowl, beat cream cheese until smooth. Gradually add powdered sugar and vanilla extract until well combined.
2. Gently fold in whipped cream until incorporated.
3. Pour the mixture into the graham cracker crust and smooth the top.
4. Chill for at least 4 hours before serving.

Fruit Sorbet

Ingredients

- 2 cups fresh or frozen fruit (such as strawberries, mango, or raspberries)
- 1/2 cup sugar
- 1 tablespoon lemon juice

Instructions

1. In a blender, combine fruit, sugar, and lemon juice. Blend until smooth.
2. Pour the mixture into a shallow dish and freeze for about 2 hours.
3. Scrape with a fork to create a fluffy texture before serving.

Almond Joy Energy Bites

Ingredients

- 1 cup rolled oats
- 1/2 cup almond butter
- 1/4 cup honey
- 1/4 cup shredded coconut
- 1/4 cup chocolate chips
- 1/4 cup chopped almonds

Instructions

1. In a bowl, mix together oats, almond butter, honey, shredded coconut, chocolate chips, and chopped almonds until well combined.
2. Roll the mixture into small balls and place on a baking sheet.
3. Refrigerate until firm, about 30 minutes. Store in the fridge for a quick snack.

Peanut Butter Banana Bites

Ingredients

- 2 ripe bananas
- 1/2 cup peanut butter
- 1/4 cup granola or crushed nuts (optional)

Instructions

1. Slice the bananas into thick rounds.
2. Spread a small amount of peanut butter on one banana slice and top it with another slice to create a sandwich.
3. If desired, roll the edges in granola or crushed nuts for added crunch.
4. Repeat until all banana slices are used. Serve immediately or refrigerate for later.

Chocolate Avocado Mousse

Ingredients

- 2 ripe avocados
- 1/4 cup cocoa powder
- 1/4 cup maple syrup or honey
- 1 teaspoon vanilla extract
- A pinch of salt

Instructions

1. In a blender or food processor, combine the avocados, cocoa powder, maple syrup, vanilla extract, and salt.
2. Blend until smooth and creamy, scraping down the sides as needed.
3. Taste and adjust sweetness if necessary. Serve chilled in individual bowls.

Honey Yogurt with Nuts

Ingredients

- 2 cups plain Greek yogurt
- 2 tablespoons honey
- 1/4 cup mixed nuts (such as almonds, walnuts, and pistachios)
- Fresh fruit for topping (optional)

Instructions

1. In a bowl, divide the Greek yogurt into serving bowls.
2. Drizzle honey over the yogurt.
3. Sprinkle mixed nuts on top. Add fresh fruit if desired. Serve immediately.

Peanut Butter Rice Cakes

Ingredients

- 4 rice cakes
- 1/2 cup peanut butter
- Sliced bananas or strawberries (optional)
- Drizzle of honey or maple syrup (optional)

Instructions

1. Spread a generous layer of peanut butter on each rice cake.
2. Top with sliced bananas or strawberries if using.
3. Drizzle with honey or maple syrup for added sweetness, if desired. Serve as a quick snack.

Chocolate Hazelnut Spread on Toast

Ingredients

- 4 slices of whole-grain or sourdough bread
- 1/2 cup chocolate hazelnut spread
- Fresh fruit for topping (bananas, strawberries, or raspberries)
- A sprinkle of sea salt (optional)

Instructions

1. Toast the slices of bread until golden brown.
2. Spread a generous layer of chocolate hazelnut spread on each slice.
3. Top with slices of fresh fruit and a sprinkle of sea salt if desired. Serve immediately.

Strawberry Ice Cream

Ingredients

- 2 cups fresh strawberries, hulled and sliced
- 1/2 cup sugar
- 1 cup heavy cream
- 1 cup whole milk
- 1 teaspoon vanilla extract

Instructions

1. In a bowl, combine the strawberries and sugar. Let sit for 30 minutes to macerate.
2. Blend the strawberry mixture until smooth. Mix in the cream, milk, and vanilla extract.
3. Pour the mixture into an ice cream maker and churn according to the manufacturer's instructions. Freeze until firm.

Maple Syrup Pecan Clusters

Ingredients

- 1 cup pecans
- 1/4 cup maple syrup
- A pinch of sea salt
- 1/2 teaspoon cinnamon (optional)

Instructions

1. Preheat the oven to 350°F (175°C) and line a baking sheet with parchment paper.
2. In a bowl, combine the pecans, maple syrup, sea salt, and cinnamon if using. Mix until well coated.
3. Spread the mixture on the prepared baking sheet in an even layer.
4. Bake for about 10-15 minutes, stirring occasionally, until the pecans are golden. Let cool before serving.

Mocha Chocolate Cups

Ingredients

- 1 cup dark chocolate chips
- 2 tablespoons instant coffee granules
- 1/4 cup heavy cream
- Optional toppings: crushed nuts, sea salt, or whipped cream

Instructions

1. Melt the chocolate chips in a microwave-safe bowl, stirring every 30 seconds until smooth.
2. Stir in the instant coffee granules and heavy cream until fully combined.
3. Pour the mixture into silicone muffin cups or mini cupcake liners.
4. Refrigerate until set, about 1 hour. Top with your choice of toppings before serving.

Sliced Pears with Honey

Ingredients

- 2 ripe pears, sliced
- 2 tablespoons honey
- A sprinkle of cinnamon (optional)
- Chopped nuts for topping (optional)

Instructions

1. Arrange the sliced pears on a serving plate.
2. Drizzle honey over the top.
3. Sprinkle with cinnamon and chopped nuts if desired. Serve immediately.

www.ingramcontent.com/pod-product-compliance
Lightning Source LLC
LaVergne TN
LVHW081503060526
838201LV00056BA/2906